# Huge Words By Huge People

---

Gently Toasted Words of Wisdom
for the Occasionally Ambitious

Also by Liam James Leaven

*On the Origins of Joy Boy's Chasm*

*Frankenstein, or The Modern Washingtonian*

www.LiamJamesLeaven.com

# Huge Words
# By
# Huge People

---

## Gently Toasted Words of Wisdom for the Occasionally Ambitious

Written by Liam James Leaven

Illustrated by Katrina Kinder

Copyright © 2024 Liam James Leaven

All rights reserved. No part of this publication may be reproduced mechanically, electronically, or by any other means, distributed or stored in any database or retrieval system without the prior written permission of the author.

ISBN: 979-8-9904716-0-3

Étienne Editions, Virginia

# Motivation

"What lies behind us and what lies before us are small matters compared to what lies within us . . .

Especially when we've just thrown down a couple chili cheese corn dogs at the hoe-down."

~ LJL and Ralph Waldo Emerson ~

"Always bear in mind that your own resolution to succeed is more important than any one thing . . .

Yes, Junior, even more important than pizza. And the remote control, yes."

~ LJL and Thomas Jefferson ~

"All that we are is the result of what we have thought. The mind is everything: what we think, we become . . .

Mmm, bubblegum. Dice. Trapeze. Funny Clown. Monkey."

~ LJL and Buddha ~

"Do not wait for your ship to come in—
swim out to it . . .

Especially when you see your gardener, Hans, sitting in the captain's chair, with your wife sitting shotgun, arms wrapped around his broad, bronze shoulders. Don't forget the dynamite."

~ LJL and Anonymous ~

"Success is how high you bounce when you hit bottom . . .

People who land on large trampolines, therefore, are generally more successful than those who land on large piles of bricks. So go get yourself a trampoline, and then hire a kid from down the street to follow you around, holding the trampoline behind you, in case you fall."

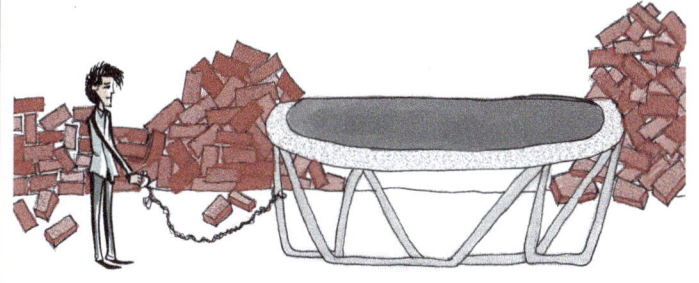

~ LJL and George S. Patton ~

"If you only look at what is, you might never attain what might be . . .

In other words, just because I am a human, does not mean I will never see my lifelong dream come true: to become a Martian."


~ LJL and Anonymous ~

"Let each day be your grand masterpiece . . .

A Jackson-Pollock-esque canvas of free-floating fears and failures, splattered melancholy and loneliness, and bouncy trampolines."

~ LJL and Anonymous ~

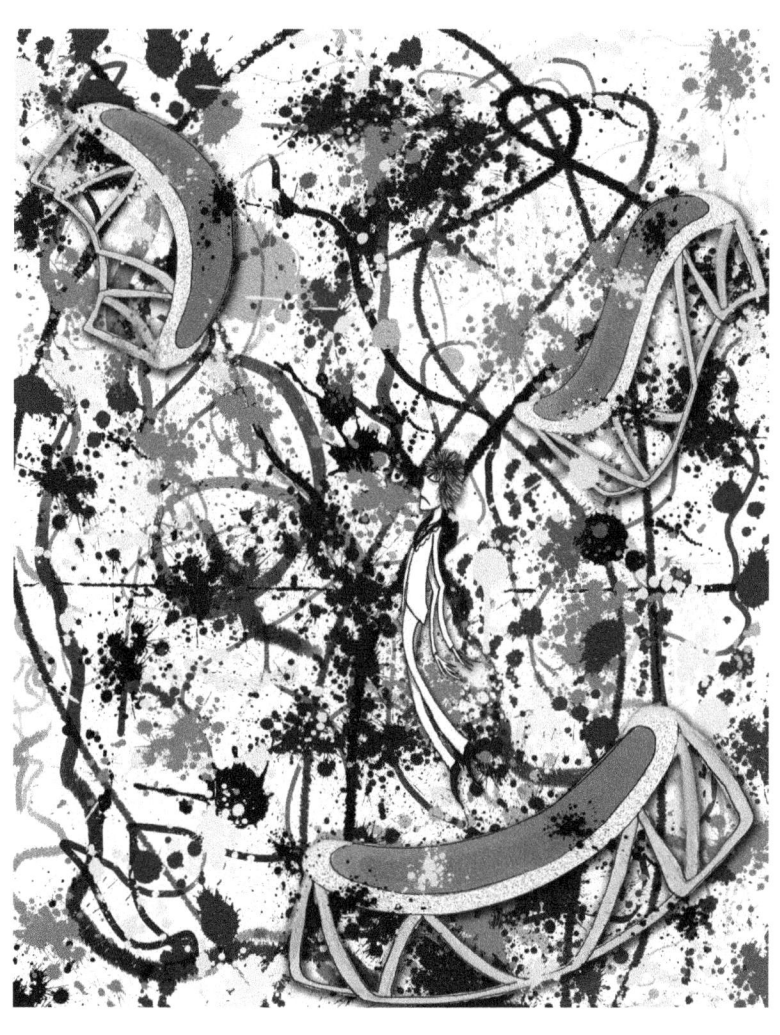

"Some people make it happen, some watch it happen, and some say, "What happened?" . . .

I respond with, "Don't look at me, man.
I've been sitting here the whole time
minding my own business, contemplating
that frog on the lily over there.
Hey man, you got a light?"

~ LJL and Anonymous ~

"The true traveler is he who goes on foot, and even then, he sits down a lot of the time

. . .

So go forward then, onward, traveler, into forever, and carry with you always a chair, for to sit upon very often, and bring with you constantly a foot, upon which to go, and last but not least have in your backpack all the time a roll of toilet paper, for with to wipe your bum, as a traveling dingleberry will grow swiftly, like a snowball that rolls downhill."

~ LJL and Sidonie Gabrielle Colette ~

"Make the most of yourself, for that is all there is of you . . .

Well except, that is, for your DNA trail. Hey, were you just down at the Fry & Grill again, gettin' on with some okra and biscuits? And it looks here like a stop at the Gas-n-Sip after . . . Trudie working today?"


~ LJL and Ralph Waldo Emerson ~

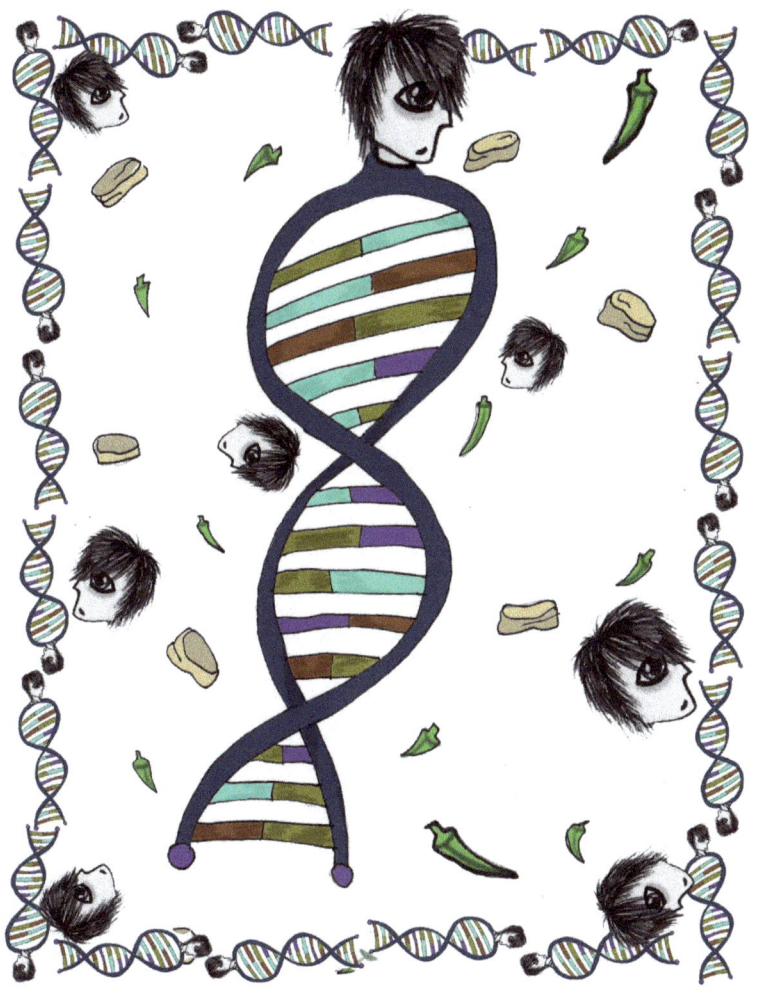

"It does not matter how slowly you go as long as you do not stop . . .

Unless, of course, your wife just found out you blew your paycheck again on the ponies, in which case you want to be sure to go, in terms of 'slow,' less slow than your wife."

~ LJL and Confucious ~

"No bird soars too high if he soars with his own wings . . .

Except, of course, for that penguin I just happened to be standing under on my last trip to the Antarctic, the one that apparently had a few too many krill for breakfast. Ever have a penguin fall on you from 200 feet?"

~ LJL and William Blake ~

"You can have everything in life you want, if you will just help other people get what they want . . .

This is why smugglers tend to do very well."

~ LJL and Zig Ziglar ~

# CREATION

"You never change things by fighting the existing reality; to change something, build a new model that makes the existing model obsolete . . .

Okay, I'm going to need some bones, a bit of skin, some modeling clay, and a spark of life. Think of all the money I'll save on couple's therapy sessions."

~ LJL and Buckminster Fuller ~

"If you hear a voice within you say, 'you cannot paint,' then by all means paint, and that voice will be silenced . . .

Oh, but first you have to cut off your ear.
And then turn the other side of your head
towards the voice. What?"

~ LJL and Vincent Van Gogh ~

"The very thing that gives you life you need to add in larger increments. . .

Hmm, in that case I'd better look up my old pal from Geneva, now where did I leave that address book? Ahh here we are, D, E, F . . . Dr. Frankenstein."

~ LJL and Anonymous ~

"Don't ever take a fence down until you know why it was put up . . . Especially if you live on a lush jungle island off the coast of Costa Rica and your neighbor is an eccentric billionaire who recently told you about the dinosaur blood he extracted from an amber-preserved mosquito he found lying around."

~ LJL and Robert Frost ~

# Leadership

"Read, every day, something no one else is reading; think, every day, something no one else is thinking; do, every day, something no one else would be silly enough to do, for it is bad for the mind to be always part of unanimity . . .

I think we can all come to our usual agreement on that."

~ LJL and Ralph Waldo Emerson ~

"If you don't like the way the world is, you change it. You have an obligation to change it. You just do it one step at a time . . .

Step 1: Get rid of all the idiots. Step 2: Close your eyes and wish real hard, like you are wishing for a pony. Step 3: Pass your remaining days rocking on the front porch with your pal, saying such things as, 'Remember when all those idiots were here, doing all those idiotic things, before The Big Wish and The Great Change?'"

~ LJL and Marian Wright Eldelman ~

"Some men change their party for the sake of their principles; others change their principles for the sake of their party . . .

Me? I'm going where the women are wearing togas."

~ LJL and Winston Churchill ~

"We have nothing to fear but fear itself . . .

Oh, and spiders. Maybe dragons, too.
Herpes. And ghosts, for instance."

~ LJL and Franklin D. Roosevelt ~

"Speak softly and carry a big stick . . .

This way, for them to hear you, they will need to come close. That's when you hit them with the stick."

~ LJL and Teddy Roosevelt ~

"Nothing will ever be attempted if all possible objections must first be overcome . . .

That settles it. I don't care how much my family keeps trying to talk me out of it. I'm joining Amway."

~ LJL and Samuel Jackson ~

# Friendship

"I don't need a friend who changes when I change and who nods when I nod; my shadow does that much better . . .

I need a friend with a lot of money and a bad memory so that each day, when I ask for 10 bucks to buy some scratchers, he will experience no déjà vu. That's French for, 'Didn't I loan you 10 bucks yesterday?'"

~ LJL and Plutarch ~

"Only your real friends will tell you when your face is dirty . . .

Like those cool cats from the party last night who kicked me in the face and then yelled, "THAT'S WHAT YOU GET FOR EATING ALL THE NACHOS AND GUMMIES!" and "P.S. YOUR FACE IS DIRTY!" when I woke up on Lexington after that wild party at Selma's. I need to Facebook them."

~ LJL and a Sicilian Proverb ~

"Beware of Greeks bearing gifts . . .

Oh olives, yes, I'd love some. My, my, and some beautiful feta cheese, you shouldn't have, Anatolius. What's that, a delivery from Priam, you say? Splendid, just place it right over there inside the wall. I do say, Anatolius, this cheese is deee-lish. My, what a large gift that is from Priam. Kind of looks like a giant . . . hey wait a minute! Damn you blasted Greeks!!"

~ LJL and Laocoon ~

"Nobody likes the man who brings the bad news . . .

So if your job title is, *The Man Who Brings the Bad News*, you probably don't have any friends."

~ LJL and Sophocles ~

# FriendBook

Info: HopelessVille, NJ
Age: Over the Hill

## Man Who Brings Bad News

Today is horrible. Like Always.
*Today*

I don't know why people even try. Nothing ever works.
*Yesterday*

Planted a garden today.

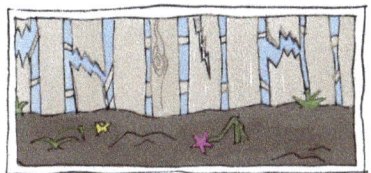

Mom!?! Even YOU reject my friend request?! What is this!!??
*Tuesday*

Man Who Brings Bad News has 0 friends.

"I can do all things through Him who strengthens me . . .

Jack Daniels, my rock."


~ LJL and Philippians 4:13 ~

"If your brother sins against you, go and tell him his fault between you and him alone . . .

If he doesn't apologize, go ahead and kick his ass. Then tweet about it. #ownage."

~ LJL and Matthew 18:15 ~

"No one can make you feel inferior without your consent . . .

Hmmm, that's strange. I don't recall signing any consent forms."

~ LJL and Eleanor Roosevelt ~

# Loss

"A little sincerity is a dangerous thing, and a great deal of it is absolutely fatal . . .

Very sincerely,
Oscar Wilde,
dead.

~ LJL and the great Oscar Wilde ~

"Perfection is achieved, not when there is nothing left to add, but when there is nothing left to take away . . .

Like when my girlfriend left and took away all the furniture and everything else with her. When everything was gone, I saw a vision of my perfect self. The giant bag of gummies I consumed on that same day? May have had a *slight* influence on the vision."

~ LJL and Antoine de Saint-Exupery ~

"If we fall, we don't need self-recrimination or blame. We need a reawakening of our intention, to be whole-hearted once again . . .

Sometimes, if we happen to fall in the right place, a good personal injury lawyer will also come in handy. I've been scoping out Grandma's Country Diner over on South Walnut Street—they always seem to be mopping around 3 o'clock. Now, where did I leave my flip-flops?"

~ LJL and Sharon Salzberg ~

"For it was not into my ear you whispered, but my heart. It was not my lips you kissed, but my soul . . .

And it was not my entire inheritance you squandered, but your future alimony payments."

~ LJL and Judy Garland ~

"Absence makes the heart grow fonder . . .

Oh, how I miss you, my super-inflated, toxic credit default swap-enabled home equity line of credit. And all the wild times you bought. Err, leased <sigh>."

~ LJL and Sextus Aurelius Propertius ~

"I once had a sparrow alight upon my shoulder for a moment while I was hoeing in a village garden, and I felt that I was more distinguished by that circumstance than I should have been by any epaulet I could have worn. . .

Later that day, when I was in front of the judge, I pleaded 'No Contest' to the charges of hoeing in the village garden and enticing a sparrow to alight upon my shoulder to act as an epaulet. Hoeing in the garden, okay, you got me. But that sparrow thing, I mean, come on Dude, that bird just came out of nowhere. And anyway, like, seriously, who made that stupid law?"

~ LJL and Henry David Thoreau ~

"What is left when honor is lost? . . .

Well, I still have my cat. Good kitty."

~ LJL and Pubilius Syrus ~

## About the Author

Liam James Leaven is the author of the comedic novel ON THE ORIGIN'S OF JOY BOY'S CHASM, hailed by Bookshop Santa Cruz as "an infectious romp guaranteed to entertain," HUGE WORDS BY HUGE PEOPLE, called a "top-shelf laughter elixir," and the comedic mash-up short, FRANKENSTEIN, OR THE MODERN WASHINGTONIAN, which takes readers on an unforgettable romp through the Nevada deserts. Get on the bus to learn more about Liam's latest projects and join him on his uproarious and insightful quest for hijinks.

LiamJamesLeaven.com

www.ingramcontent.com/pod-product-compliance
Lightning Source LLC
Chambersburg PA
CBHW040413070526
44119CB00139B/185